Play and Talk with Your Toddlers

20 Research-Based Creative Activities That Will Get Your Kids to Laugh, Play, and Speak More.

Publisher's Note

The publication is designed to provide accurate and authoritative information regarding the subject matter covered. It is sold with the understanding that the publisher is not engaged in rendering psychological, financial, legal, or other professional services. If expert assistance or counseling is needed, the services of a competent professional should be sought.

Copyright © 2020 by Audrey B. Carmela
Published by JW Consulting LLC

Proofread by Cheryl Williams
Cover & Interior Design by John Barrow

We support copyright. Copyright fuels creativity and encourages diverse voices, promotes free speech, and creates a vibrant culture. Thank you for buying an authorized edition of this book and for complying with copyright laws by not reproducing, scanning, or distributing any part of it in any form without permission. You are supporting writers and allowing us to continue to publish books for every reader.

ISBN 9798698399414
All rights reserved.
Printed in the United States of America

For Bowen,

my extraordinary partner in life and work

Table of Contents

Why This Book?

Do you want to develop your toddlers to be a great communicator but only find that they shy away from speaking? Or do they get easily annoyed because they have trouble expressing their wants and needs?

You get frustrated, and you start searching:

"When do toddlers talk?"

"When to teach a baby to talk?"

"How to get a toddler to talk?"

Search no further. This book will give you plenty of research-based guidance and step-by-step activities to get your toddlers to speak and make it fun for both of you too!

Why this book?

With research-proven strategies and easy-to-follow fun activities for toddlers, these 20 activities make an ideal home school companion during a particular time like this. Here are what you can expect:

- 20 fun speech routines designed to motivate toddlers to think, communicate, and play
- A simple guide that turns professional language development into child's play
- Research-based strategies to stimulate toddlers' abilities to express needs and desires
- Practical strategies that will help you transform daily activities into excellent opportunities for communication and play

- Easy-to-follow instructions with step by step guide to help you stay mindful and maximize opportunities to communicate
- Guided exercises to create little crafts and develop speech capacity through hand-on experiences
- Practical ideas and strategies to troubleshoot development setbacks and get prepared for preschool life

Should I read it?

This book is ideal for beginner mommies and daddies and even those who are just preparing for their first kid. It is also an excellent resource for early childhood educators, caregivers, speech therapy scholars. If you are one of those lucky grandparents, you will get lots of inspiration from this book as well, so you can have a memorable time with your grandkids.

So, stop worrying, and let's have some fun and create some memories together!

Introduction

Welcome! New mommies and daddies!

First of all, congratulations! Now you must have one or more little angels running amuck in your home! Look at their little faces and waving hands! How adorable they are! Let me guess, are you picking your way through the debris, strollers, bottles, dirty clothes, diapers, toys? On your littered domestic landscape, are your little angels having so much fun?!

I know as new parents, you are probably having piles of plans of where and how to start this life journey with your little angels, so exciting! Let me guess, on top of all that, you are interested in jumpstarting your toddler's speech because you've picked up this book, right? If so, even better, this is the right choice for you!

This book was written to help both your kids and you. New parents, just like you, can use this book to accelerate kids' communication and playing skills through some exciting and practical activities. These activities are categorized into different stages and times. We have also designed them specifically for children aged eighteen to thirty-six months. Younger or older children can also find this book helpful depending on themselves). Both you and your kids will feel comfortable and excited to follow.
On the other hand, it is also designed to be user-friendly for you, busy parents. This book also includes various strategies and techniques to help you interact with your kids and boost their language development, emotional expressions, and playing skills. I'm sure everyone will be happy with it!

Since many children attend preschools early, we've also
provided details about preparing your child for this big
move. Trust me, it will be exciting!

Thank you so much for picking up our book. It will be
a fantastic experience to go through this process as new
parents, watching your kids start to smile, listen, talk,
understand, and express their feelings. Let's jump into
this journey!

Part 1: First Thing First

Chapter 1: Why Speaking?

Language is everything. We use words, phrases, and many sentences to communicate with others every day. Think about it. We watch TV and listen to the radio. We laugh when we hear what we hear and enjoy talking about our lives with others. We use language all the time, and language makes our lives simpler and more enjoyable. Language allows us to do a lot of things. We use language to make decisions, attract audiences, express our feelings, compliment others, ask for support, play with others, seek love, ask for approval, make friends, advise, apologize, and so on.

Think about the time when you were picking up a foreign language. You got really excited when you have learned a few simple words or phrases because that just made the process smoother. You were getting closer. Learning many new comments and trying to fit them in sentences to actually make it mean something can have so much fun. At this stage, your kids learn how to use words to make sense of their world, too. They want to use words to make some demands, get some help, or express their excitement to this new world (Gaines & Missiuna, 2007). There are several different language development phases, from using single words to using complete sentences and paragraphs to telling stories. You are about to learn to help guide your children to the next step in their language development. If your kids have already learned to use some single phrases, that's awesome! Keep going as there is always so much more to explore!

Chapter 2: Guidelines

You've probably heard about this. There are many strategies that you can use to encourage your kid's language development. And actually, a lot of them sound like common sense — you probably are doing them now without realizing it! They are designed to create opportunities for your child to speak in a natural, low-pressure environment. We don't want to make this language learning process a painful experience, just like how you feel about exams back to high school. This will make your kids feel overwhelmed or under pressure. You won't like that, so let's use these strategies with mindfulness and moderation.

Just talk

This will be the most straightforward one. You can just talk about what you are doing, seeing, eating, or thinking about when your kids are around you. Yes, random talk with just simple words, only talk so your kids can listen with or without intentions. Something like "Ok, I just finished washing those dishes, now, I'm going to dry them, then it's all over." Again, remember to use simple words, especially when your kids are young, so they might tend to follow in their heads. Keep your sentence short as well, just like "washing dishes," "drying dishes," and "all done."

To make it a bit more fun for you, you can also talk about what your kids are doing, seeing, or touching if they are playing (O'Brien & Nagle, 1987). In other words, you will sit around and tell them what they are doing, something like, "Look at Bob, he is walking around now. He picked up a blue shovel and put it in a mini truck!"

Using this "talking strategy," you do not expect your kids to respond to or even mimic what you're saying. But this will leave them with some impressions, more or less. Please do not have too many expectations that your kids can automatically mimic or repeat after you. This strategy is just giving your kids an introduction to language during their playtime and everyday activities (Girolametto, Weitzman, Lieshout & Duff, 2000). This can help children realize that talking is natural and fun. If they're actually following and repeating after you, that's great!

Repeat and expand

Here is how to adapt this strategy, just repeat what your kids say, especially crucial phrases that you feel like they are trying. If you repeat it, this will give them some affirmations and confidence to mimic back. Research shows that children who tend to mimic will deliver faster and more significant improvement in their language development later. When they hear your repeat, It also encourages them to continue the rest of the conversation and learn about the basic turn-taking that we use when talking to others (Paul & Elwood, 1991). Practice makes perfect. It's essentially the same thing with repeat. The more a child talks hears, and repeats, the stronger sense he or she can get. If your kids say "Tiger!" repeat it again. "Tiger! "The child may repeat it again. "Tiger!"

Now I'm going to talk about this strategy in two different ways. One way is for you to repeat what your kids say. The other is to tell a phrase in your way as an adult. It is essentially the same thing but only to repeat what your kids said and expand it to a longer sentence. This is a very traditional and effective way to connect with your kids — you may have already done it. But make sure you don't complicate things. It's just a simple sentence that can make them try to understand and learn to say it later on.

A rule of thumb is to expand their sentences by no more than three letters to start with. If your kids say "cat run" when watching a cat chasing a ball, you could say, "You're right! The cat is playing. Your kids could also say "blue car" while they saw a blue vehicle on the street. Your response might be something like, "The blue car it is." You can make your expansion a little longer if you feel your kids learn things fast, like, "The blue car is parking along the street."

Also, think about this way. Suppose you can follow the conversation led by your kids. In that case, they are more likely to be interested and inspired to continue the conversation. Pay attention to what your kids are doing, listen to your child's say, and expand on it. They're going to be more interested in having a conversation with you if it's about what they want and what they intend to say. If your child says "CarGo," do not try to speak to them about something irrelevant, like the teddy bear you have found next to you. Join the talk in the car! Try adding, "The car is going fast! "Do not overwhelm your kids with too many different words when you expand. Expanding one or two words will be just fine. If your kids are very interested in a bug on the wall, don't try to slap on the bug, this is a part of their learning process, join them. If they point to it and say "bug," you might want to go along with the subject. Comment with something like, "The bug is black and moving fast."

Open up conversations

When you only connect with your kids in a yes or no question, you will only get one-word answers! Open-ended questions can better encourage your kids to expand their vocabularies and make them try to explore more ways to respond to the problem (Nemeth & Erdosi, 2012).

When you do something, especially watching something along with your kids, ask your kids to explain what they see. Try something like this, "What's the dog doing? "Instead of," Will, the dog, go to eat? " Make the question open-ended rather than something like, 'Do you want to watch the dog drinking water?", Try this way, "What do you like about the dog?"

Also, offering choices allows your kids to respond in a broader range. This can let your kids know that language is an essential tool that can be used to influence the world later on. Giving your kids control over the language will make them feel more comfortable using the language and enjoy its benefits. Try something like, "Do you like a banana or an apple? "Which allows your kids to choose, to practice their vocabulary, rather than just," Would you like an apple?" "Is the dog staying there or running away?" See?

Your options don't always have to be fixed. Choose some other stuff like the content in books or stuff on TV. It encourages your kids to participate in a discussion by giving them a small range of choices of how to speak it out. Like "What's the dragon doing? "I know this can be a bit tricky for kids at such a young age, so if you see your kids shrug or look confused, try to limit the range of choices in our question. "Is the dragon feeding or running away?"

Did you ever remember how much more attentive you were as a child when the adults around you began talking to each other in their ways? Everything was strange to you, right? Thus, changing your voice as you have your kids around will attract their attention and add excitement and fun to your conversations. Use various tones in your voice or change your voice; speak with a loud voice or a hushed whisper. And explain your voice to your kids. "This is my loud voice," Encouraging them to mimic your voice can be a lot of fun.

Support when things are slow

Minimize the pressure

Minimize the stress and expectation you put on you and your kids in this process. Have you asked too many questions? If this is the case, replace that with a simple comment. For example, instead of saying, "What is it? "While pointing to a picture, simply talk about what you see in the picture: "I see a big elephant." This way, you don't leave your kids with a direct question or put too much pressure on them. Keep the process mindful and enjoyable. Give your kids more encouragement if they made some progress.

Add support

Provide all kinds of support when you see your kids are showing vital interests and trying hard to express themselves (Nugraha, et al., 2019). Show them some images, point to something, use gestures, and amplify sounds and phrases to highlight things as you can (Elbow,1987).

Just slow it down.

Slow down the conversation. Children who are just getting started to learn a language cannot understand what you say if you say it too quickly (Nemeth & Erdosi, 2012). Just imagine you are trying to learn a foreign language with an instructor who speaks way faster than you can follow up, now you get the point.

Make it short

I've discussed this before, but it's worth repeating again and with patience. If the kids just focus on one word when you say two or three, then do not make long sentences with five or six words. Don't hope that the kids will repeat with a similar one because they have already forgotten what you said!

Relax

Give the kids enough time to explore, to feel, and to try. As they learn by exploration, so did we when we just started. Provide them with enough encouragement and patience to try and work things out on their own. Move forward or step back with them as they do, so they won't get upset. How do you know that an activity is too challenging for a child? If your kids get frustrated, this may signify that they are overwhelmed or simply did not understand it. Stop from here to make it easier, or just give another try tomorrow, if you feel that your kids are no longer having fun.

Part 2: Make It Fun!

Activity 1: Paint Everywhere

What we need

Multicolor sidewalk chalks

A place that allows you to draw things with the chalk

Let's start

Let's just start drawing! You can usually start by
drawing a huge circular, a plain square, or other simple
figures. See what the kids are doing and how they react
to it. Show your kids two or three pieces of chalk
simultaneously, and several colors if available.

Now let your kids draw something just like you just did.
Say what they are doing with some short,
straightforward sentences. Like "You drew a circle!"
Or "Look at the circle!". Wait a minute for them to
respond and realize something. After they have done
creating their own figures, say how amazing they are,
show your enthusiasm for their work.
Just a reminder, please draw something easy to figure
out and follow, like a sun, a ball, or a face. If you
remove your face, name your eyes, your nose, and your
mouth. After you finish drawing, show it to the kids.
You can even color and repeat some similar patterns of
drawing.

Wrap it up

Let your kids finish drawing his last piece. Announcing the end of the activity by saying, "Time to clean up." Start singing a clean-up song if you can. Let them help you get the chalk out of here. Give them a container and see if they can open it on their own. Set it up in a way that they may struggle with it a little bit. Pause and wait for them to figure it out on their own, then join after a few minutes if you can see they've tried hard enough. Your goal here is for the kids to indicate that help is needed.

Guide your kids

Offering choices: Say, "Do you want black or pink?" Or "Would you like to draw a circle or a square?" Show your kids what it looks like by doing it yourself too. This is about saying something for themselves to figure out their needs or things they want.

Follow the lead of the kids: Mimic the actions of the child. If they start drawing lines or circles, just do the same thing after them. Narrate the stories of the child in a simple but animated way. If they point to their artworks or just stand up and say something about it with their words, acknowledge that by saying something about what they refer to (e.g., "Oh, how nice!" or "I like it").

Gestures and some stupid sounds: if you draw a dog, make a barking sound; if you draw a cat, make a meowing sound; if you draw a cow, make a mooing sound, etc.

Activity 2: Playful Kitchen

What we need

An empty shoebox or other square containers

Some dried kidney beans and dried pasta,

Spoons, cups, and other kitchen utensils with no sharp edges

Small cookie bits (anything that can be covered under the beans)

And If your children are in the stage of exploring things by putting things into their mouths, be careful not to let them eat anything that could cause danger.

Let's start

Show the box of beans and pasta to your children. Play with the beans and encourage them to do the same thing (pay more attention to what they are doing with small things in this activity). Many children enjoy touching, digging, and putting their hands under the beans. Give your kids some time to feel their new toys here and encourage them throughout this process. Follow the lead of the kids, and do the same thing as they do.

Now take one of the utensils and use them to pick up and pour some beans, and keep talking about what you're doing in simple words like "I'm picking the beans up, then I'm pouring them down." Next, give the

kids a spoon. Watch what they do with it. Taking turns
with some other utensils (don't use a knife, please)

You can lead each turn by saying, "It's my turn ... now
it's your turn," or "Now it's Bob's turn." Then pick up
another utensil into this process. Most children find this
activity very enjoyable and relaxing, just like they love
to play around on the beach. Once all the utensils have
been used, hide cookie pieces or other small toys under
the beans and pasta.

Wrap it up

End the activity once all the utensils have been used, or
your kids have found all the stuff. Sing a clean-up song
and clean things up together as you do in other
activities.

Guide your kids

Self-talk and parallel talk: Talk about your actions and
the move of the kids. for example, "I'm mixing the
beans" or "You're touching the beans."
Improvise your sentence depends on the child's existing
language skills.

Pause: Give the kids some time to process the
information and respond to it. You might say, "I can't
find the cookie," or "I can't see the pizza." Then count
to five and wait for the kids to respond. Some of them

would start to look for hidden items. If there's no
response, just keep playing.

Activity 3: Farm Life

What we need

Farm animals—cow, horse, sheep, goat, pig, rooster, or just a cat or dog, and a barn

Let's start

If you don't have animal toys, just draw them down on paper, cut them into individual characters, and put them on your table. Make the animals greet each other by saying "hello" or "hi," or by making some animal sounds (e.g., the cow says "moo," the sheep says "baaah," or the horse says, "neigh-neigh"). Keep it relatively simple, and let your kids take turns after yours. Sometimes, after the kids mimic your actions, they will tend to imitate your speech.

Once the animals have finished greeting each other, make them walk in and out of the barn and say, "Knock, knock" to pretend to open the barn's doors. After the kids get it, pretend to feed some food, and make animals play around, and go to sleep, or even go to the potty! Following a routine that the kids can relate to similar routines in their life will help them understand the activity better.

Wrap it up

End the routine before the kids lose their interests. Just
tell them that the animals are sleeping and that you
don't want to wake them up, and we can play them
again later. Return characters back to their original
places.

Guide your kids

Offer the kids some choices: For example, you might
ask, "Do you want a cow or a sheep?" Or "Should the
animals eat or sleep?" And pause three to five seconds
after a comment or question to give the kids some time
to think and react to it.

Self-talk and parallel talk: Narrate your actions and the
actions of the children. For example, when you say,
"The cow is sleeping." Children who don't talk or
respond to it, make snoring noises or display one or
two words like "sleeping" with your finger pointing to
a cow sleeping in the barn. Improvise the type and
length of the sentence based on the child's language
skills.

Activity 4: Bubbles!

What we need

A bottle, with a solution to blow bubbles

Paper towels or washcloth to dry hands

A hula hoop or a small circular round item to blow
bubbles through

Let's start

Open the bottle while you say something like "open" or
"pop the bubbles," then dip the wand into the solution
while you say "dip in." Feel free to improvise on the
child's comprehension and skill.

Since some children might have trouble blowing
bubbles, we shall start by making the toddler capture or
pop bubbles (It's a way to develop the child's playing
skills). Ask your kids whether they want a vast bubble
or a small bubble. Be playful and pay attention to their
interests, and add a lot of joy and inflection to your
voice.:

Take turns blowing bubbles (say, "my turn," "your
turn," or "Mike's turn" to emphasize). Encourage your
kids to pay attention to this game. Make this as a
routine, and see if your kids will imitate you. Get them
to blow the bubble onto your hand. Then let them blow
the bubbles that can rest on the wand. If the kids are
still struggling, that's all right! Don't push it too much.

You can try blowing kisses so that they are more aware that their lips are involved in blowing. Rounding lips can be difficult for beginners, so don't expect it to be absolutely perfect at first. Take your time and let the process flow.

Wrap it up

If your hands are wet, point it out (e.g., "You've got wet hands, I've got wet hands too!"). Children who don't speak or understand much, say "wet hands" when pointing at the wet hands. Clean your own hands with a paper towel or a washcloth. Next, give your kids a paper towel or washcloth. See if they need some help from you. Help your kids if you see that they are struggling with it.

Guide your kids

Self-talk and parallel talk:
Narrate your actions and the actions of the children (e.g., "I'm drying my hands," "drying," or simply "drying"). Improvise the type and length of the sentence.

Ask a bit, not a lot: For example, you can say, "There's a bubble" (first comment); "It's a big bubble" (second comment); "I'm going to blow another bubble" (third comment). After three words, ask a question like, "Do you want more bubbles? "For older children who can understand some differences in size, ask," Do you want a giant bubble or a small bubble?

Use somebody's languages, point to the bubble, or say "bubble," "big bubble," or "small bubble" if they don't respond after a few seconds.

Pause: Give your kids some time to process the information and react. For example, you can say, "This is a big bubble." Then count to five and wait for the kid to say something. If there's no response, don't force it, just keep playing.

Activity 5: What a Ball!

What we need

Any types of ball that are soft, such as foam, cloth, or plastic ball that can be picked up and played smoothly by children

A large plastic bowl or bucket

Let's start

Show the ball to your kids, explain with simple words like "Ball!" to understand.

Now you can bounce the ball up and down and say "bounce." Look at your kids and then show them the ball and say "bounce" or "I'm bouncing the ball." See what they are doing with the ball.

After your kids can understand and play with it for a while, roll the ball and say "roll" or "roll the ball." Look at your kids, and then give it to them, and say "Roll." Let them try to roll the ball back to you. Continue this routine, and let them take turns by grabbing or dropping the ball in the large plastic bowl or bucket. Keep going with this routine. If your kids don't want to follow your lead, that's fine. Follow their leads if they are still interested in the play, and every time you have a ball, just make sure you make a specific action and repeat it until your kids pick it up. You can even use their favorite toys to attract them better.

Wrap it up

End the routine with a singing voice, say, "Bye-bye, ball" as you wave your goodbye, and then move on to something else.

Guide your kids

Question a little bit, but not a lot: For example, you can say, "Here's a ball" (first comment); "It's a big ball" (second comment); "I'm going to bounce the ball" (third comment). After three words, ask a question like, "What do you think? Or What do you want" "Say this while holding the ball up to the kids? Pair your words with some body language for better understanding. If needed, point to the ball or say "ball" again if your kids don't respond after a few seconds.

Expand: Remember, this technique should be used in moderation because you want a natural conversation instead of pushing them too much. The kids say "ball," so you can say, "Yes, that's a big ball," or "Bounce the ball," or "Roll the ball." When you're expanding, make sure you keep your kid's original intentions as good as you can.

Sentence completion tasks: after repeating the word ball a few times, make a comment like "I have the ball" while holding the ball, or say, "Do you want the ball? "Just before handing it over to the kids.

Part 3: Make My Day!

Activity 6: Good Morning!

A song is an excellent way to set up a routine or habit and create language development opportunities. Using a song to greet your kids in the morning as they wake up, will give them the chance to practice their language in a friendly, relaxed, and comforting way (they might learn to mimic and say the same thing back to you later on)

A good idea here is to make your own song to say hello to the morning. You can choose to copy the tune from a song you are familiar with, Such as the "Happy Birthday" song. Change the words to reflect the activity you and your kids are doing as the example below. You can also search online to find something you like.

Good morning song -- from "Happy Birthday."
"Good morning to you, Good morning to you, Good morning my dear baby, Good morning to you."

Activity 7: Play at Breakfast

Breakfast can be a rush time for a family. If you're too busy to prepare and get ready for the work, you can skip this. You can just go with other activities and core strategies we talked about before to bring language development into your daily routines. If you happen to have some extra time in the morning or take a day off, you shall try some of them.

What we need

Let's talk about what you're having while you're having breakfast with your kids. For example, you can mimic what you saw on TV to describe the taste, color, and smell of the milk you are drinking, just in simple words! Or just merely talk about how you cook the food, put a burger together, or crack the eggs! Involving your kids into something is also a lot of fun for them. For example, you can let them be in charge of stirring pancakes, saying, "Look at you, you are stirring this big, lovely and soft pancake!" Also, give them some attention and interactions, especially when they show some interest in what you are eating, cooking, or how the food looks.

Let's start

You can even make breakfast together. Here are some fun breakfast ideas for you and your little ones to make together:

1. Fruit and cereal.

Cut a piece of strawberry or any other fruit for your cereal. Ask your kids to put some of them into the cereal. Give them some motivations and speak out their actions, something like "strawberry in!", "Look, the cereal is smiling at you!", Or "There's one more staying in the dish!"

2. Pancake.

Cut the fruits and put them onto your pancake to decorate the pancake on purpose. my favorite one was to make the pancake look just like a smiling face, and turned to my kids and said: "He's smiling," "He's so happy! "Or, "He wants to know if you are doing well!"

Wrap it up

You can also simply make comments on the food you're eating together. This will give your kids some impressions and even let them reflect on this when they have something to eat later on. So, use this opportunity to expand the language of your child. Use simple adjective words to describe the way your food tastes and how they look like. For example: "This is such mushy oatmeal! " Or "I just love sandwiches with lots of bacon like this one." If they show a lot of progress, later on, you can even ask your kids questions like" What do you like the best about your breakfast?"

Don't let your kids sit there while cleaning up dishes and trying to get them involved. Communicate with them with things such as "It's such a big mess, right?" or "Let's clean up this sticky table!" This is another opportunity to give your kids some simple tasks. such as turning the faucet on and off and say, "Water on, water off!" You can also flip those ending up songs in previous activities into cleaning up pieces. Just like this:

"Clean up, clean up, everyone everywhere."
"Clean up, clean up, everybody does the share."

Activity 8: Dress Up!

What we need

Getting a toddler dressed can be challenging! If you're just trying to get your kids dressed and get them out of the door, it might be turned into a painful process, especially in some rush mornings. (Well, most of the mornings). So, when you have some spare time in the morning on weekends, why don't you try to convert it into one of the activities that you can play with your kids? Then this can become an everyday ritual without feeling like a task.

We all know the risks of letting your kids decide what they want to wear in a day when they feel excited about almost everything. Unless you're ok to let them wear their Halloween costumes every day and keep running in your house. So, here are some ways to help you if you want to:

Pick out a few clothes that you are comfortable with the night before. (Don't complicate this, it should not be the way that most of the mommies decide what to wear in the morning)

Let's start

Then, show them to your kids the next day they wake up, let them pick the one that they want to wear if they can. Just take it slowly without overwhelming your kids since they just get up. If they choose one of them, ask them why to see if they can feel something about it, just like "It's pretty! Do you like it? Why did you pick this one?". If they have trouble picking from these, help them a bit by saying, "Look at this pick one!" "Here's the blue one you may like." Or "How do you like this one with half blue, half white?"

Wrap it up

After they finally pick something to wear, you can have some fun now. Many children enjoy being stupid or seeing others acting silly. You can try to put the one they picked for themselves on you. Encourage them to tell you why they start to laugh and ask them what's wrong with it. If they don't know at this moment, help them seek where the problem is in a simple phrase, such as "Do you think it's too small?"

Or, you can play the trick on them, try to put your toddler's clothing on them in the wrong way, such as on the wrong body parts. Put socks on their hands, or put their gloves onto their feet. It will be a great way to get them to learn both clothes and their bodies and encourage them to tell you where the right position is.

Guide your kids

One way to get dressed up for a game is to turn it into a race later on. If your kids can get themselves dressed up most of the time, they can compete against you as you also dress up in the morning. You will let them pick their favorite clothes, then lead the game, like, "Shirt now!" And "One more sock to go!". Speak out each piece of clothes on your own, too, as you dress up to encourage them to imitate you and make the game more exciting. Another fun option is to race against a song that plays as the background and encourages kids to dress up before it is over.

Activity 9: Colors

No worries, you don't actually need a painting kit with pencils, paints, and other supplies. Paper bags and several colored pencils can be just enough for kids to have some fun.

For developing their language with coloring, simply talk to your kids about the colors you're using. For example, "I've got a red one." Also, try to describe what they're using when taking their turns to pick their colors. You can say, "Nice! You've got the blue pencil." Or "What red paint! Do you like red?"

Also, just a reminder, it's always a great thing to get kids involved in color projects such as painting to develop their sense in multiple layers. So, let your child be color-creative. If they're going to pick a yellow, let them pick yellow! If they insist on choosing the black, let them go with black! Perhaps you have a future Picasso in your house already! Also, keep talking about what you're painting while drawing something like a demo for your kids. Like "I'm going to draw a little horse. He's handsome and has blue eyes. (doesn't matter if you are a bad artist) When your kids come up with some responses such as" horse" or "blue horse," You can expand that as "You are right, it is a blue horse with a long tail!".

If you know that your kids can say something more, they get used to speaking just one or two words and encouraging them to talk more. You can do that by asking an open-ended question, such as "What kind of horse do you think it is? What is your horse doing?" As adults, we tend to enjoy the open-ended question ourselves, such as "Tell me about your new phone," Or "How do you like that show?" This provides us many opportunities to answer in multiple ways. Your children will appreciate this too.

Activity 9.1 Paint with Water

What we need

Water and a brush (or your fingers)

I know it's exhausting to clean up all the mess after painting. No problem, this "painting activity" will also let your kids have some fun without getting things messy. And one more good news is materials are basically free: just get a brush (or your fingers) and a bowl of water.

Let's start

The steps are also easy just as following:

- Give your kids a brush and a bowl of water.
- Go outside where there's a side wall (maybe just in the backyard of your house).
- Dip your brush into the water. Tell your kids what you are doing, something like "make this wet," "Let me pick up the brush," and "I will draw on this wall later."
- Use your wet paintbrush to paint on the sidewall or on the side of the house.
- (If it's not too hard for your kids, explain why the water will disappear after you finish it, just get a little bit science involved)
- Draw several things in different shapes and sizes, explain to your kids, such as long, short, round, square, flat, or thin.
- Let your kids try this and let them tell you what they are painting and how they like it, using our strategies talked before.

Activity 9.2 Sink and Float

What we need

A couple of toys in different materials, a bowl of water

This is a fun way to learn about water! If your child can be quickly getting excited about water play, please don't do it before sleep. Let's jump into it:

Let's start

- Take a large bowl and fill it all the way up with water, grab some small toys, and other waterproof stuff with you. Things that you can pick including marbles, leaves, a rubber duck, a sponge, some hoops, and rocks, anything that is small enough to fit in the bowl (except your phones)
- Pick a place nearby that you won't worry about things getting wet, such as the backyard behind your house.
- Sit down with your child and try to put toys you brought with you into the water. it's better to pick some that can float and some that will sink down to the bottom)
- Demonstrate to your child what sink and float mean by giving a few examples of each. Simply explaining with "Look, rocks are going down to the bottom." And "See, sponges are just staying on top of the water!" Repeat this for a couple of times so the kids might tell what is up and what is down.
- Then, let your child guess if it's going up or down, before you put items into the water, and

allow them to try themselves. "It's up, wow! "
Or " It's going down, look at it!"

- Then, explain that things going up are things
  floating. Those going down to the bottom are
  things sinking; they are not too tricky, so let
  your kids try to say that, and offer some help
  with pronunciations. For example, if they say
  "fo" for float, simply repeat "float" afterward.
  You don't need to correct their accents. Just
  repeat the word for them to follow and repair
  themselves.

Activity 10: Night Night

Activity 10.1 Pictures in A Day

Just taking some pictures in the day.

We all enjoy dinner time, which is precious as mommies, daddies, and babies can sit around and have a big meal in peace after a busy day. Many of us are used to sharing our day. One of those fun ways to do it is to help your child talk about his day by getting him some pictures to share. This practice is an excellent way to introduce the idea of sequencing. Sequencing means being able to retell something that has happened in the same order of how it happened, including the beginning, the middle, and the end of it. This activity is also an excellent way to practice all the words and sentences they have learned, their abilities to re-organize things, and share their experiences. You can pick a day, use your phone or camera to take pictures of what they are doing with you or without you in the day. Taking three or four pictures will be enough for them to start with.

After you show these photos to your kids, ask your kids: "Look at this, what have we done here?" Or "You look happy with this little doll, what are other things you found interesting today?" Allow your child to explain what's going on. It could take a few minutes to think and express themselves when your kids need help recalling an activity or speaking out a sentence. Stay patient and give them some motivation and side assistance. "You recall that you played with the toys, right? What were you building?" If your kids respond with just one or two words, such as "play car," try to

expand his sentences. You can let him repeat with some
more reminders of other activities that he was
interested in.

44

Activity 10.2 Bath Time!

You must have tried to take your kids to a shower, as you can see, bath time could be turned into a stressful time for their involvement. Some kids don't like playing with water, while others love it. Either way, if things get out of control, there will be a huge mess left behind in there. Be sure to follow your child's lead — don't push it too much if they don't like it (While don't drive them too excited even if they love it). Encourage your kids to play in the water for a proper amount of time if they're having fun (don't let them be there for too long if they get cold!). You can keep it short if they don't like it anyway. Just keep in mind, water can also be dangerous. Never leave your child alone in the water even for a few seconds!

Bath time is a perfect time for your kids to develop their skill sets, not only in language learning but in all aspects of development, including cognitive, social, and emotional skills. For example, playing in the water can help your children develop their problem-solving skills. As they play in there, they tend to seek what's going on and why. Water helps improve the child's motor growth by encouraging them to actually play the water by pouring, splashing, and squirting. This also helps provide your kids with sensory experiences as they explore various temperatures. Other than all that, spending time in a hot tub can help reduce stress. There are lots of benefits and lots of fun! Below we found you some exciting activities during the bath time.

Bath time songs

Singing is excellent for promoting the development of languages. The classic "Rubber Ducky" song was our personal favorite during the bath time for our kids. Another one popped up in my head is "Itsy Bitsy Spider." For some of you, you can even try "Splash Splash I was taking a bath." When you repeat the same song several times in a row, your children will get acquainted with the tune, letting them fill in some of the words of their choices. You may even start singing a song and then pause to wait for your child to encourage them to jump in.

The game of splash

Water games are also great for kids to have new experiences and learn some new concepts. By educating your child and showing them some hands-on examples, you can let them have a more realistic understanding of what's going on during bath time. Here are some examples you can use:

Run the water. Let your kids get a sense of temperature when you run the water. While the water is flowing, test it to make sure it's ok, then put your child's hand into it. Ask them whether they feel the water is too cold, too hot, or, just right? You can ask your kid, "Is the water hot? "If your kids are just getting too excited without thinking about it, that's all right! Only repeat the correct answer to confirm with them again.

When the water fills the tub, let them gently step into it, feel how the water covers their leg, knees, chest, etc. The feeling of their bodies covered by water in the bathtub helps your child generalize some basic concepts. Ask them how they feel about it and how they like it.

Now your kids are probably just getting excited and playing with the water, try singing "splash splash" as they make small splashes with their hands in the water. Ask them to describe the water if it's deep or shallow to them? If they can't tell, no worries, say something like, "The water is going low. It's almost all over your body! " to let them realize.

When it's time to get out, just say, "The water is too cold now!"

Activity 10.3 Time to Sleep

It's time to get ready to go to sleep! (I know, what a day!) Here are some of my favorite activities to wrap up the day and get your kids to sleep.

Songs of Goodnight

We all love songs! Don't worry about it. If you are not good at it at all — you can customize it in your own ways. Some of the classic songs you can flip are "Rock-a-Bye Baby," "Twinkle, Twinkle Little Star," "You Are My Sunshine," and "Hush, Little Baby." You can easily find all of these songs on YouTube and make your own songs out of them.

While you have sung for a while (and your kids still have their eyes open). Encourage them to sing along with you. Or have your kids jump in during the middle of it. Make sure you sing in a calm, slower, and clear way so they can follow and even understand most of it. For example, "You are my sunshine, my only —" pause right here so that your child can follow with, "Sunshine!"

Also, I know most of you have already known this and even are doing it yourself. We believe that reading to your kids is one of the best things you can do to make it easier to develop their language skills. The task is also a great way to help your child calm down at night. There are many, many storybooks to choose from, especially some good bedtime storybooks. Don't be afraid to read the same ones again and again. This could become a ritual to your kids that its bedtime, and it could also motivate them to remember it and mimic it.

Part 4: Think & Grow

Activity 11: Magic Towel

Three or four miscellaneous objects (e.g., puzzle pieces, blocks, or crayons)

A towel that can cover all of them

Show those items to your kids one by one. Hold up and say, "I've got a cow" Or "I've got a car" (pause for three seconds); "I've got a car" (pause for three seconds). Next, play with the items you showed to your kids. Make a cow moo, drive the car back and forth, and have the cow beep. Do whatever come to your mind. And always let your kids join the play whenever they want to.

When you feel like the kids have become familiar with these items, take the towel out in front of them, and tell them that it's a magical time! You can either say to the baby that you will cover these things with a magic towel to make them go away or cover them up. With the items covered by your towel, take one of the things out without having the kids seeing it. Then flip the towel and say, "Ta-dah! " Let them see the remaining two and then ask what happened to the other one by saying, "Here's the car. Here's the truck. Where's the cow?

Wrap it up

After taking a few turns, just say that a magic towel
needs some rest. Let the kids help you put the
remaining things back to where they were. Your kids
might keep asking and thinking about it all the time.
Let them practice this themselves to see if they can
figure it out. Otherwise, repeat what you did and
explain that the towel has magic that can make things
go away! I know this sounds like cheating or lying, but
once the kids find out, it will be fun and a great
thinking and observing process.

Guide your kids

Question a little, not a lot: For example, you can say,
"Here's a cow" (first comment); "Here's a truck"
(second comment); "Here's a car" (third comment).
Cover the items with a magic towel and remove one of
the pieces. Follow up with the question, "What's
missing?" Let them guess and think for a while before
you move on.

Pause: pause three to five seconds after a comment.
Give the kids some time to process the information, and
then respond, encourage them to think and say
whatever they feel might be the reason. For example,
you might say, "I'm covering these pieces of the puzzle!
Bye-bye, cow, man. Bye-bye, truck, man. Bye-bye,
car." Say this while covering every piece by the towel.
Then pause for a second and wait for the kids to say

something. Don't push if there's no response. Just keep going, since this is an activity that needs some understanding and thinking for the kids.

52

Activity 12: Puzzle Time

What we need

Some pegs or chunky puzzles

Puzzle pieces that are related to a category (e.g., farm, transportation, or ocean), just some simple ones

Let's start

Get the container in front of your kids, take pieces of the puzzle out from it. I usually keep the parts of my puzzle in a wooden box. Show one or two pieces of them at a time, let them have the chance to review everything you get, and ask them how they like the puzzle. If they are confused (which is normal), you shall explain how it works as "They look like this because we are putting them together into an interesting picture!" Both you and your kids shall start to try to put them together next. If you feel they are struggling with it, provide assistance by letting them see how you are doing it or just say, "Look at that pattern over there! That looks like a deer but without the left leg, look at what you have, is it a leg?" They will probably understand how this works in this case.

Continue to complete the puzzle. Just to add some fun, try to mimic each animal's sounds or vehicle on the puzzle at the same time when you two are getting pieces together. If it's an animal puzzle, if you can, also talk about where the animals live, their habits, or what they eat (e.g., "Dogs eat bones" and "Bunnies eat carrots"). A lot of knowledge and information like this can be delivered to your kids throughout communications. Some of them will leave them deep impressions.

Wrap it up

When your kids have finished playing everything and enjoyed their work, it's time to wrap things up. Help the kids remove the puzzle pieces by playing a comfortable, fun game with him. For example, you can ask them this "Where's the chicken? "Or," I can see a horse. Did you see that? " And " Hmm ... where's the fire truck?". Do this for every piece until all the pieces are found and put into the box.

Guide your kids

Sentence completion: When you are holding a piece of the puzzle, say what it is, educate your kids on that, and see how your kids respond. For example, "I've got a pig."

Then, after repeating two or three times, do it again. but stop right before the word pig, and let the kids finish the sentence: "I've got a... " If the toddler needs some hints, give a bit more information just like "I have a p ...." Give them a few seconds to respond and say "pig," and if they don't say anything, repeat the word and keep playing.

Oops: As soon as the kids get familiar with the puzzle, once you play several rounds with them, you can try to put the pieces in the wrong positions, then ask them for help, give them a chance to correct it, which will leave him a more profound impression and the feeling of achievement.

It's best to start with a completed puzzle, to begin with, if your kids have never done this before with you. This way, your child will have a bigger picture to reference where the pieces are going to. Then he can remove those pieces just one at a time and bring them back together.

Those puzzles that are not simple groups of animals or cars usually have a matching picture of the puzzle tray's design. It can also be useful resources to train the kids to identify the correct spot for each piece. Their ability to imagine how the whole thing might look like and put them together that way can trigger more communications and guidance you can have with them. The more you interact, the more and quicker the kids will learn.

If your kids get frustrated quickly, just use puzzles with fewer pieces or larger pieces. I've found that when a child struggles to learn a new language or a new thing, it's best not to focus on just teaching shapes, numbers, and the alphabet. Because these principles are not yet applicable to the level of the child. And they don't really help your kids to express themselves by just teaching them "one, two, three," Or "A, B, C."

Activity 13: Scavenger Hunt

What we need

One or two miscellaneous items

Let's start

Until the kids get the hang of it, hide just one item at a time. Show the thing and name it. Next, tell the kids that you're going to hide it. Tell them not to look at it and follow you, demonstrate this by covering your eyes as you say it "No peeking" or "No looking at me." Then quickly go to hide the item, saying, "I'm hiding this doll and will be right back." By the way, don't hide the thing under some heavy stuff or next to furniture with sharp edges for younger kids. For the first round, keep it in some open areas without too much difficulty being easily found. For example, just put a doll on a corner of the sofa so that your kids can find it in only a few minutes to better understand the game's nature.

Follow the kids when they are trying to look for the item, communicate with them in this process, "Where is the doll? "And they might respond with "I'm looking for a doll," encouraging them a bit in this process if they totally miss their ways, as "you can look around in that way."

It's ok to take them a while to get used to this activity. You may want to add more dramatic acts and moves to make it more fun. Such as putting your hands on your forehead, keep your eyes wide open when you're looking for it with them. Children love this kind of dramatic action, particularly if an adult does it along with them! When the kids finally find the thing, acting as you are super excited and yelling, "You've seen it! " Following by clapping. When the kids have found the items a couple of times in the next few rounds, you may want to let the kids hide the item this time, and you will look for it. Give them some suggestions and point out a few places for them to hide the item. Repeat this routine.

Wrap it up

After the kids have enough fun with it and both of you might feel tired now, let them know that it's time to take a break and we can have more fun the next day, such as taking them to a nap, having lunch, or just letting them have some rest with you.

Guide your kids

Ask a bit, not a lot: For example, you might say, "Hmm ... I'm looking for a cow" (first comment); "I'm looking underneath the couch" (second comment); "I'm looking under the table" (third comment). Then you may say, "Where's the cowhiding? "Say this when you're acting in some dramatic ways to keep the kids feel interested in this activity.

Expand: Probably not in this activity if your kids just focus on finding the stuff and are attracted by the surroundings, if the toddler says, "Cat Hide," then you should say, "Yes, the cat is hiding somewhere." Just keep the conversation in the same directions to let your kids talk to you when they can still focus on what they are doing.

Body languages: This can be more helpful sometimes than just keep saying, and more comfortable for your kids to understand and get entertained, such as we mentioned above, simply placing your hand on your forehead while you're looking for it. Or scratch your head and keep your eyes open widely, just like you are thinking very hard along with them. When they finally get it, you shall act as you get really excited by saying, "Wow, nice job!" Or "Here you go!"

Activity 14: My Feelings

Emotional intelligence is something that we continuously hear about recently. It's the ability to perceive, regulate, and convey feelings. Studies have shown that children with high emotional intelligence are actually more cooperative and chattier at school, making school life more comfortable, safer, and happier.

Here we're going to explore some ways to help your kids express their thoughts and feelings. This may be one of the most essential skills for a child to develop at such a young age. As our kids are learning how to speak at this moment, they sometimes don't have the right word or language to explain what they have experienced and how they felt. Like mommies and daddies, we need to jump in to guide them through this. This is also a big part of language learning and development. Helping them talk about their feelings will give you the chance to broaden your child's vocabulary and teach them how to convey their feelings appropriately.

Emojis

There are lots of emotions in us as human natures. Sad, happy, angry, excited, irritated, anxious, jealous, and more — no wonder a child can't keep them all straight!

Think of as many different words as possible that you can talk with kids about emotions. Think about drawing pictures of faces with those words. It is a perfect way to develop your kid's emotional language and keep the process simple and joyful. (I used to print emoji from my phone!)

Help them say it out

We will have negative feelings in our life, more or less,
even if we just stay at home. There are many ways to
help your kids realize, think, and learn about them.
Sometimes, when children are getting upset or mad, it's
hard for them to just say it with words. Instead, we
shall use parallel talk as a question to teach them the
names of various emotions they have. When your kids
cry because their brother took their toy, you might say,
"Hey Tom, you are mad because Johnny took the ball,
right?" Or "Tom, tell me what happened? Are you mad
because Johnny took your ball?" You may also use
parallel talk to explain the reason they feel that way. "I
think you're sad because you accidentally dropped your
toy, and it is broken! " It gives them the word, the
reason, how to associate the feelings with some words,
and how to say it, as they need.

It's also a good idea to use your feelings as a
demonstration, expressing how you feel with the
emotion's name. For example, "I am excited to go to
the zoo!" or "I am so frustrated because I forgot my
purse at home!" Or use someone else too, "Look, she's
sad because she just took a fall." This way, you can
help them recognize the feelings of others, also.

Dance it out

Music is an excellent catalyst for expressing,
encouraging your kids to "dance their emotions" and
express themselves through the lyrics' movement. This
can help them vividly understand different kinds of
emotions. Just play a song and motivate your child to

dance how the music makes them feel. You'll need to lead this activity at first so that your child will get it. An upbeat song might make them dance quickly and happily, while a slow song would make them dance slowly and sadly. Have your child follow your lead for each song. By telling them how each lyric makes us feel, always encourage them to give you any feedback.

Play it out

Kids love to learn by playing. Putting emotions into their playtime will help your kids understand feelings actively and allow them to practice their understanding of emotions. You may use some toys they like to demonstrate it. For example, an elephant toy may say to a teddy bear, "I'm mad at you, bear! I was going to eat the cookies, and you ate them all!" Show your kids how you can fix the problem. The bear may say, "I'm so sorry. I'm going to give you some more to make up for it,'" and the elephant is happy again! "Thank you, bear, that makes me feel good!"

Understanding the emotions expressed by facial expressions can be challenging for kids. Still, it's essential for us as adults as part of the body language, allowing people to quickly understand and respond to each other. Help your child learn this skill by playing this activity:

- Make an exaggerated face, sad or happy.
- Let your kids guess what kind of emotion is under that face.
- Naturally, they will need some assistance to figure it out, use the choice-making strategy. "Am I happy or sad, huh? "It will give your

child a smaller range of options to choose from and make the process less overwhelming.
- "Now it's your turn." Let them make an exaggerated face for you to guess what it is.
- When your child can recognize something simple like happy and sad, ask them questions like, "What are some things that make you feel happy?" And take the lead by saying, "Daddy is happy when he gets a nice shirt" or "Mommy is upset when she gets a flat tire."
- Take pictures of their emotional expressions. Using your phone or camera to take photos of your child's faces: sad, happy, and angry. Have fun sharing a story about why they feel that way, and you can always play this with them later on. Let them tell you what happened behind that picture and how they felt.
- Enjoy yourself. If things worked out great for both of you, your kids would enjoy making crazy faces. Just do the same thing, and it will give you some laughs.
- At the end of it, tell your kids to draw a face that makes them feel happy (or some other emotions). Encourage your child to describe what happened behind their feelings. This can be turned into a story sharing activity later on!

Activity 15: Read A Book

Talk about reading

We can't say enough about the value of reading with your kids. According to the American Academy of Pediatrics, reading with children or to your children can effectively promote early brain growth. It also develops literacy skills, which in turn will have a positive effect on your child's language skills and future academic success. Studies indicate children who have the habit of reading a lot or listen to their parent's reading have more excellent vocabulary and even math skills later on. We can see, the more you read together, the more words they know, and the better their language skills will be, just like self-learning.

It's a good start by reading to your kids every day before sleeping or when they are resting, even if it's only two or three minutes. This will also give you a chance to connect with each other on a one-on-one basis. It's not about the contents and finishing the book. It's about creating meaningful and interactive experiences with kids!

Interacting with the book

When you read a storybook to your child, you'll want to show your kids how to appropriately interact with books. For example, start by speaking out the title, the author, and the book's illustrator. Move your finger along the content to display how the text goes from left to right. (It doesn't matter if they can't read at this moment or write words, just give them the sense). Show your child the correct way to hold a book and how to read it. When you read the stories, especially some exciting conversations, read them slowly and clearly, and add some comments followed by open-ended questions "So Tommy and Susan are trying to pick some apples from the tree, can you imagine what that looks like?", Or "The little bears are chasing each other, and playing near the pond, with some ducks swimming there, how lovely it is, can you imagine what other animals are also there with them?"

It's essential to pick a time that you are not in a rush, like a bedtime or before dinner, to read together. To start with, just select a picture book with fewer words. Flip through the pages of pictures and tell them what you see on there. Your kids may try to picture the characters, scenes, or even a specific story theme in their heads. Highlighting the characters when you are reading as characters are the ones bringing a story to life. Try your best to use different ways to show your kids about what you see. from other facial expressions, body language, to dress styles of unique things from one character to another. "What does Tom do?" "What do you think of Pete?" Or "What do you think will happen next? " Some of those questions can trigger more interest in the kids and let them actively imagine what is going on in the story.

About the book for your kids

Depending on the development of your children, there are plenty of books to choose from. Choose what you believe is best for your kids. If your baby is still at the ripping pages stage, a board book or a soft book could be a better option than a paper book. Let your kids pick the book that is interesting to them. You may explain what it is about by looking at the description. And if they want a book that's at a higher level, that's fine. Let them explore for you to read to your children, here is no need to read everything in a book; just look at the pictures and talk about what you see!

Also, talk about how to use the book, the way to keep it. A fun way to do this is to open the book upside down and get your kids to correct you. When your kids point out that the book is upside down, say, "Ah! We're keeping the book this way!" This can give them some basic sense of a book, preparing for their future readings.

Tell your kids to turn one page at a time, saying, "so we're not going to miss any of the stories. You don't want to miss Sam, Lucy, and other friends, right?" When the pages are paper that is fragile, tell them about how paper books can be easily torn off, so it's essential to be careful when turning the pages.

Make it interesting

Some younger kids might have trouble sitting for a very long time. Let them perform the story when you're reading it. Allow them to feel as they are in it as well! Select any exciting authors. It's better to pick those books that allow your kids to experience various emotions, characters or connect in many ways. You can even follow your kids' lead if they show a firm intention to perform the story based on their understandings and imaginations.

Another way to keep their interests is to read in a funny voice. Children prefer to listen to some stories that are funny and full of humor. You can try different voices for each character. Make your voice louder and exaggerated when the character is angry, lower the voice when the character is sad, etc.

If your kids have a favorite book, it's all right to read it several times. This will encourage them to remember the plot, understand it, and help you tell the story next time you do it again. It's a perfect way to learn and form a sense of language and plot in their heads. Let them take the lead to finish reading for you this time. You can even "make a mistake" when reading the book, and give them a chance to correct you.

Part 5: Ready for Kindergarten?

Activity 16: Bingo Markers

What we need

Washable bingo markers

Plain paper or coloring books

Let's start

Show your kids two or three bingo markers. Give him one that is not opened. If the kids fail to open it but are still trying in a wrong way, such as pulling the marker instead of turning it, ask them, "do you need some help?" If they do, teach them how to open the quality first. Draw a few strips or random patterns on the white paper, and tell them, "here is a flower (Or whatever you drew)." Now let the kids take the marker and draw whatever they want if they simply repeat after you and tell them they can do something differently.

After your kids are comfortable using bingo markers, you two can take turns drawing patterns in different colors from other markers. You may now get a color book with some simple contents, just like animals, various types of flowers, or colored painting. The same thing as what you did in the previous puzzle activity, just get involved with your kids together, tell them they can use whatever colors they think that will suit the painting or the color book, take the lead by painting on your own and describe what you are doing: "Here's a rose, so I would like to use the red marker for its leaves, and then, what color do you think we should use for the stern?" Getting your kids involved by asking their opinion like that. And after you have finished several paintings with them, let them take the lead. Pick whatever they like and use colors whatever they think are suitable for pictures. Some explanations like "Steve, how do you like this one?" And "What do you think the color is on the roof?". Let the kids practice and feel the fun of turning the combination of different colors into lovely paintings throughout their understandings. You can try to find more coloring books to give them various experiences. Keep having those conversations with your kids to guide them through by themselves, and express what they feel about things, and always cheer them up if they have trouble finishing a painting. Encourage and praise them after they finally finished painting. There is no right or wrong!

Wrap it up

End this activity when you feel the kids are losing their interests or just getting bored.

Guide your kids

Talk through the activity: Talk about their choices, what you are doing, ask what they feel like things, how they feel like their choices. Improvising the form and length of the sentences depends on your kid's language skills.

Give them some options: In this case, "Do you want to use red or blue? "Do you want to color the dog or the

cat? "Encourage some answers from them by saying,
"You like little cats, do you want to try the cat?"

Don't pick too many markers with all kinds of colors,
so that your children won't get overwhelmed, and they
might think out of the box to ask for other colors. For
children who like to use the same color (some do!),
encourage them to try something different. ask if they
would like a new marker, or simply say, "I think your
roof can be in some other colors, maybe you want to try
dark green this time?"

Activity 17: Pictures and Patterns

What we need

Pictures of your kid's favorite characters and patterns cut from magazines (five to seven should be good to go)

Stickers to stick the photo onto a board or a wall

Let's start

Put the patterns or pictures on the table. Tell your kids what's in there. For example, suppose it's a photo showing you were at a pool. In that case, you can say, "Mom is swimming," Or if it was a birthday party, you should say "Bobby's birthday party," or it's just some flowers: "It's a pretty flower." Take turns with the kids, and hear their comments about what's in the picture. And then ask your kids which one they like, let them pick one for the next move.

Give your kids an unopened sticker, see how they will deal with it. If they can peel to open it, then great! If they cannot open it, keep going until they say "help" or "open." Some kids need help holding things, especially here we have several pieces before they put it on there, ask "now let's put the stick onto the picture we are holding, can you teach me?" If they choose to put the sticker on the front side, then let them! Show them how it looks by placing the picture onto a wall. "Can you see anything from this site?" They will understand what's going on and correct themselves. If they have trouble holding the picture, help them hold the image and let them put the sticker onto the backside of it.

After all, the photos have been stuck onto a board or a wall. Make a big fuss about it, something like, "We're all finished! Good job, Mike" Then let your kids help you clean up, move forward to some other activities.

Guide your kids

Let your kids talk about what is in the picture once you put it onto the wall. If your kids say something that is not related to it, or they misunderstood the question. For example, if a dog is in the picture, they say, "Here's the cat." You can say, "Where is the cat?" see if they can notice the mistake.

Follow the lead of the kids: imitate their behaviors. When looking at all the photos before starting to play with them, give them enough time to carefully look at those photos.

I strongly recommend that you use a picture of your kids like the most. Choosing their favorite ones would make your kids feel happy and have stronger motivations to finish it, and they will be more likely to show off what they have done!

Activity 18: Make an Instrument

We all enjoy singing songs or listening to music by the little ones! Have you ever tried to make some simple instruments with your kids? There are many music-related words and knowledge you can use and teach your babies in making these. You can use words like colorful, noisy, shake, blow, hum, sing, drum, beat, loud, quiet, soft, and others to describe the instrument you are making together. It's also interesting to make some sounds with alternative syllables, such as "ba da ba" or "doo be doo be doo." Be dumb, and have fun! Even try to hold a family "concert" with your brand-new instruments! Here are some easy ones you can try out together:

Activity 18.1 Make a Maracas

What we need

Plastic Easter Egg

Some dried beans

2 plastic cups

Some colorful tapes (such as scotch tapes or colorful washi tapes)

Instructions:

- Open the eggs and fill one half with the rice or dried beans. Close it back up tightly.
- Place the egg between the heads of two spoons and wrap the tape around the spoons and the egg to keep it in place.
- Tape the bottom of the spoons together as well to make a handle. Make sure to tape it tightly— you don't want the rice to fly out!
- Shake out a beat!

Activity 18.2 Make a Drum

What we need

Safe scissors (kid's version)

Some construction papers

markers, paint, or stickers

canister with a lid

Tape

hole puncher (optional)

yarn (optional)

Instructions:

- Cut a piece of construction paper that will fit around the width of the canister.
- Have your child decorate the paper using markers, paint, stickers, or whatever you have!
- Wrap it around the container and then tape it on securely.
- If you want to make a strap so your child can hold the drum in front of them, punch holes in the drum's side and use yarn to make a strap.
- Drum away on the top of the lid!

Activity 18.3 Make a Guitar

What we need

Markers, colored pencils, stickers, or other decorative things

Empty tissue box

Rubber bands

Instructions:

- Decorate your box.
- Slide the rubber bands around the box, so they're going across the opening of the box.
- If available, using rubber bands with different widths. Those different sizes are going to make different sounds.
- Strum away!

Activity 19: Sensory Play

As the children grow up, they learn about the world through their senses. By integrating sensory play into your child's daily activities, you will provide stimulation for all five senses. It also gives them the vocabulary to communicate their experiences. It's hard to talk about something they haven't seen or experienced before. When engaging in sensory play, you can incorporate language to talk about what they're experiencing with their senses.

Activity 19.1 Sensory Sticks

What we need

Children's safe scissors

Items with various textures (sandpaper, cotton ball, pillow, towel, etc.)

Glue

Popsicle sticks

Instructions:

- Cut your textured materials into strips.
- Glue them to the Popsicle sticks.
- Let them dry.
- Feel each different texture with your child. Talk about smooth, rough, soft, fluffy, bumpy, and whatever else you feel.

Activity 19.2 Toilet Roller Binoculars

(Make colorful toilet roll binoculars that you can have some fun afterward)

What we need

2 toilet rolls of paper

Duct tape

Hole Puncher

yarn

Stickers, labels, other decorative items (optional)

Instructions:

- Tape the two rolls together. You can use colorful duct tape to help make the binoculars brighter, but it isn't necessary.
- On each side of the binoculars, punch a small hole (one on each roll).
- Tie a piece of yarn through both of the holes. The yarn should be long enough to hang around your toddler's neck.
- Decorate with stickers, markers, and other decorative objects.

Activity 19.3 Pumpkin Bottle

(This activity will allow you to make a super cute craft that is ideal for Halloween. There's a lot of vocabulary you can use for this one too. Think about Halloween, pumpkins, tearing, hair, nose, mouth, base, orange, black, and so on)

What we need

small plastic bottles, such as an empty water bottle or soda bottle

child-safe scissors (optional)

orange construction paper

black Sharpie

Instructions:

- Tear off the labels from the bottle.
- Tear or cut up strips of the orange construction paper.
- Fill the plastic bottle with the orange paper strips, so that the bottle appears to be orange.
- On the outside of the bottle, use your Sharpie to draw Jack O'Lantern's eyes, a nose, and a mouth.
- If you wish, you can paint or color the cap green to make a stem.

Activity 20: Preschool Prep

Talk about preschool

At this age, you might want to start thinking about preschool. Kids start preschool at different ages actually, but generally between three and four years old. Kids will generally understand some basic instructions and have some vague sense of the environment. They are also able to ask questions to fulfill their needs and obey the rules. Consider chatting with professionals in your local kindergartens to better understand requirements and things to be aware of.

Don't worry if you think your kids might not be ready for kindergarten based on what I just said above, the preschool will still be great to help them grow faster. Preschool provides children with a great environment to learn things in a much formal way. Such a domain can be both socially and academically, with other kids learning and playing together at a similar age. Preschool encourages the development of language and cognitive skills. Children have a better chance to reach much more vocabulary than they are exposed to at home. Cognitive skills, such as abilities in problem-solving, asking questions, and understanding reasons, are also being focused on in preschool. It's never the wrong choice!

Make the transition to it

Let's talk about it

Speak casually and festively to your kids about preschool before it begins. Just say it as a new and exciting place with many friends playing together, there's nothing to worry about. Take the time to check out the preschool location, reviews online, the directory of faculties, and children's picture books from it if available. You can take the opportunity to introduce some new vocabulary and concepts to your child. talk to them in a way that can make your kids feel excited and look forward to it. (which is true if you pick a great preschool, so mommies and daddies, please do your job here)

Feel free to talk about the activities that kids may like to participate in or the things they might want to see. Don't forget to tell them about preschool rules — be polite, take turns, and share things. Practice these rules at home, mostly taking turns and sharing things.

Establish the right schedule for it

Get your child into a daily routine that can perfectly fit in the preschool schedule. Help your kids stay with the schedule, especially during the night, and wake up in the morning, around 2 months before preschool starts. Routines like this make your child feel comfortable and easy without feeling overwhelmed all of a sudden. An evening routine can help your child relax in peace, and a morning routine can help your child be well prepared for a new day. Consider reading some bed storybooks for your kids when they feel anxious at the beginning. Ensure your kids have a lot of sleep and rest before they go to preschool, particularly if they have morning classes. Practice some other language skills like "after you," "thank you very much," "may I," "excuse me," or "sorry." probably, you've already done this part. Anyway, with some simple practices during the day, to give them a basic sense of how to act properly.

Regular chores

In preschool, children are also expected to clean up after themselves. Encourage and practice this at home. There is a list of clean-up songs to sing while you and your child pick up their toy, clean up their dishes, or just get their laundry in order. Sometimes preschool kids have a role for the day, such as a line leader, doorkeeper, snack helper, or song singer. Teachers tend to let them take the turn, so they can have equal chances to practice. One way to prepare your kids for this is to encourage them to help at home. Let them hold the door for you sometimes, and then praise them. "Thank you for keeping the door for me!"

Visit the Preschool

If necessary, have a visit to your child's future preschool before you officially send your kids over. Let your kids see what preschool looks like, how they feel about the environment, get to know their teacher, shake some hands, and understand what to expect (yes, this is your first time). You can chat with teachers about some basic things, then show your kids to let them be aware of in advance, such as show them where the toilet is, when the snack time is, and where the playgrounds are.

Plan Social Activities

If you can, plan and practice your child's social activities at home to learn how to share, take turns, and play well with other children. It may be anything small, like setting up a carpet with other children, taking music lessons together, sharing candies from their teachers, or cooperative activities in crafting classes. Try to understand more by asking their teachers directly or visiting their websites.

School supplies for them

We love to shop for all kinds of stuff, now it's time to get some school supplies. Everything will be brand new and colorful, and all the pencils are sharp! (be careful of that). Find out what your kids need to carry lunch, snack, and/or school supplies at preschool. Then you can take them with you, going on your mini field trip to a store that sells school supplies to enjoy the shopping. (now probably you need to do it online for safety issues)

Before taking off, write a list of items you need to buy for your kids. Talk about everything as you write it down to your kids. After your list is made, let your kids count the things on your list and look at details to see if they need something else. You can give this to your kids and let them take the lead in the shop.

Thank you

Congratulations on getting through this whole 20 activities. You could have picked from dozens of books on teaching and helping your kids speak, but you took a chance and checked out this one. We believe you've made a great choice!

If you find this book helpful, please take a moment, leave a review, and share it with your friends. Your suggestions and satisfaction are the greatest motivation for our efforts now and in the future.

We feel honored to have put our best efforts to support you and your spouse on this beautiful journey!

Reference

Elbow, P. (1987). Closing my eyes as I speak: An argument for ignoring audience. *College English, 49*(1), 50-69.

Gaines, R., & Missiuna, C. (2007). Early identification: are speech/language-impaired toddlers at increased risk for Developmental Coordination Disorder? *Child: care, health and development, 33*(3), 325-332.

Girolametto, L., Weitzman, E., Lieshout, R. V., & Duff, D. (2000). Directiveness in teachers' language input to toddlers and preschoolers in day care. *Journal of Speech, Language, and Hearing Research, 43*(5), 1101-1114.

Nemeth, K. N., & Erdosi, V. (2012). Developmentally Appropriate Practice for Infants and Toddlers. *Young Children*, 49.

Nemeth, K. N., & Erdosi, V. (2012). Enhancing practice with infants and toddlers from diverse language and cultural backgrounds. *YC Young Children, 67*(4), 49.

Nugraha, A., Izah, N., Hidayah, S. N., Zulfiana, E., & Qudriani, M. (2019, March). The effect of gadget on speech development of toddlers. In *Journal of Physics: Conference Series* (Vol. 1175, No. 1, p. 012203). IOP Publishing.

O'Brien, M., & Nagle, K. J. (1987). Parents' speech to

Paul, R., & Elwood, T. J. (1991). Maternal linguistic input to toddlers with slow expressive language development. *Journal of Speech, Language, and Hearing Research, 34*(5), 982-988.

toddlers: The effect of play context. *Journal of Child Language, 14*(2), 269-279.

www.ingramcontent.com/pod-product-compliance
Lightning Source LLC
Chambersburg PA
CBHW031322130726
47988CB00007B/2942